# THE UNTAMED WORLD

# Giraffes

## E. Melanie Watt

RAINTREE
STECK-VAUGHN
RSVP® PUBLISHERS

A Harcourt Company

Austin   New York
www.raintreesteckvaughn.com

Published by Raintree Steck-Vaughn Publishers, an imprint of Steck-Vaughn Company.

**Library of Congress Cataloging-in-Publication Data**

Watt, E. Melanie.
    Giraffes / E. Melanie Watt.
        p. cm. -- (The Untamed world)
    Includes bibliographical references (p.).
    Summary: Describes the physical characteristics, behavior, and habitat of giraffes.
    ISBN 0-7398-4971-9
    1. Giraffe--Juvenile literature. [1. Giraffe.] I. Title. II. Series.

QL737.U56. W38 2002
599.638--dc21

2001048143

Printed and bound in Canada
1234567890  05 04 03 02 01

**Project Coordinator**
Heather Kissock
**Project Editor**
Lauri Seidlitz
**Raintree Steck-Vaughn Editor**
Simone T. Ribke
**Illustration and Layout**
Warren Clark
Bryan Pezzi
**Copy Editor**
Jennifer Nault
**Photo Research**
Joe Nelson

**Consultants**
Mona Keith, Senior Giraffe Keeper, Calgary Zoo, Calgary, Alberta, Canada
Clive Spinage, Wildlife Ecologist, Oxon, United Kingdom

**Acknowledgments**
The publisher wishes to thank Warren Rylands for inspiring this series.

**Photograph Credits**
**Calgary Zoo:** pages 19, 20, 23, 24T, 59, 61; **Corel Corporation:** cover; **Giraffe Manor:** page 55; **Giraffe Project** (www.giraffe.org): page 45; **Marion Kaplan:** page 54; **Carol Peterson:** pages 4, 5, 9, 10, 12, 15, 21, 25, 26, 29, 32, 34, 36, 42, 51, 52, 57, 60; **Clive Spinage:** pages 8, 16, 27, 38; **E. Melanie Watt:** pages 6, 7, 11, 13, 17, 18, 22, 24B, 28, 31, 33, 35, 39, 40, 41, 43.

# Contents

# *Introduction*

**Giraffes are the tallest land animal in the world.**

*Opposite: From the neck up, a giraffe can weigh 500 pounds (225 kg).*

*Africa is known for its exotic animals, including the giraffe.*

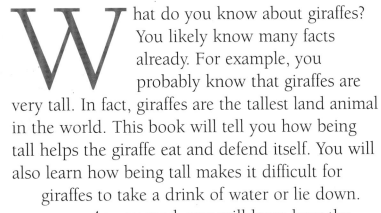

What do you know about giraffes? You likely know many facts already. For example, you probably know that giraffes are very tall. In fact, giraffes are the tallest land animal in the world. This book will tell you how being tall helps the giraffe eat and defend itself. You will also learn how being tall makes it difficult for giraffes to take a drink of water or lie down.

As you read, you will learn how the giraffe's body is unique in many ways—from its hooves to its horns to the end of its tail.

You probably also know that a giraffe has an unusually long neck. Do you think this means it has more neck bones than you do? Read on to discover the answer! You will also find out what it means when two giraffes are **necking**, why their tongues are purple, and why giraffes whistle. You will learn how to spot signs of giraffes in the wild, what makes them sick, and how they help birds called oxpeckers. Turn the page and get ready to learn about the amazing giraffe, inside and out!

# Features

**A giraffe is easily recognized by its long neck and legs, large size, and special color pattern.**

*Opposite: With its long neck and legs, the giraffe towers over the treetops.*

Take a look at the picture on this page. Would you ever mistake a giraffe for any other animal? Probably not. Giraffes have many unique features. A giraffe is easily recognized by its long neck and legs, large size, and special color pattern. If you look closer, you will see two or more hornlike growths on its head, and large, dark brown eyes with long lashes. A giraffe's sloping back makes its front legs appear much longer than its back legs. In fact, its front and back legs are about the same length. The giraffe has large, heavy feet with two hoofed toes on each foot. A short-haired mane grows along the back of a giraffe's neck. Its long, narrow tail has a tuft at the end.

*Due to their size, giraffes rarely cluster together. Even when resting, they stay about 20 feet (6 m) apart.*

# Size

Just how tall is a giraffe? Bulls, or male giraffes, are larger than cows, or female giraffes. The average height for bulls is about 17 feet (5.2 m), and for cows is 14 feet (4.3 m). The tallest giraffe ever recorded was a bull that was 19.3 feet (5.9 m) tall. By lifting its head up and sticking out its tongue, a giraffe can add an extra 3.5 feet (1.1 m) to its reach.

Even young giraffes are big. At birth they are about 6 feet (1.8 m) tall and weigh more than 150 pounds (68 kg). Adult male giraffes are often heavier than adult females. An adult male usually weighs between 1,760 and 4,250 pounds (798 and 1,928 kg), and an adult female usually weighs between 1,210 and 2,600 pounds (549 and 1,179 kg). Adult giraffes' tails are about 27 to 40 inches (69 to 102 cm) long and have a tuft on the end.

## LIFE SPAN

Giraffes can live to be more than 30 years old in captivity. In the wild, they rarely live longer than 25 years.

*The giraffe's height is its main defense against predators, allowing the giraffe to spot danger from far away.*

# Skin and Coloration

Giraffes have very thick skin. It can be up to 0.6 inches (15 mm) thick on their shoulders and is about 0.3 inches (8 mm) thick on their neck. Thick skin may help protect them from parasites, or it may just be natural for an animal this large. The muscles attached to the giraffe's skin are not well developed, making it difficult for a giraffe to shake its skin like a horse.

*Some giraffes have broad-patterned markings, while others have smaller patterns. Markings differ between the subspecies and individual giraffes.*

Giraffes have patterns of light to dark brown markings on a cream-colored background. The underparts of a giraffe are usually light in color and unmarked. The blotchy pattern can get darker with age. Each giraffe's pattern is unique. This pattern can be used, like human fingerprint patterns, to tell individual giraffes apart. A giraffe keeps its pattern for life.

Although they are not common, there are white giraffes as well as giraffes that are almost black. There are even a few giraffes that are completely tan-colored, with no creamy background.

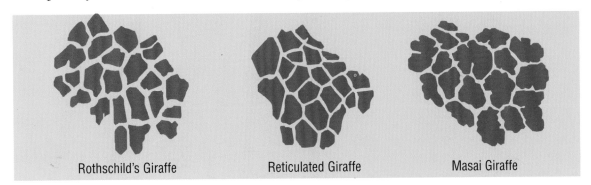

Rothschild's Giraffe          Reticulated Giraffe          Masai Giraffe

# Special Adaptations

Giraffes have many special **adaptations** or features that help them survive the challenges of their environment.

## Neck

The giraffe's long neck is its most obvious adaptation. The giraffe uses its long neck to reach food found high in the treetops. Like most mammals, the giraffe has seven vertebrae, or neck bones— except the giraffe's are much longer. An adult giraffe's neck is about 6 feet (1.8 m) long. Extra-strong neck muscles support these heavy bones. Specially adapted joints on the back of its head allow it to raise its head straight up. This lets it reach even higher for leaves.

## Respiratory System

A giraffe has very large lungs. They are needed to move used air all the way up its long neck and out of the giraffe when it exhales. Inside a giraffe's neck is a windpipe that moves air from its nose and mouth to its lungs. If the giraffe did not have such large lungs, it would breathe the same air over and over from its windpipe.

*Its height allows the giraffe to eat leaves that are beyond the reach of most land mammals. Only the elephant can reach as high.*

# Circulatory System

A giraffe's heart is more than twice as big as scientists would expect for an animal its size. It must be powerful to pump blood all the way up to its raised head. A giraffe's heart is about 2 feet (0.6 m) long and weighs about 25 pounds (11.3 kg). It beats about 150 times per minute. This is very fast. Usually the larger the animal, the slower the heartbeat.

Along with its large, hard-working heart, a giraffe's **circulatory system** includes many special blood vessels that help control blood flow. One way these vessels do this is through one-way valves. A one-way valve is a flap of skin that will only allow blood to move in one direction. When a giraffe lifts its head up quickly, one-way valves prevent blood from rushing away from the brain, which could cause the giraffe to faint. When the giraffe's head is held low, one-way valves in the neck keep too much blood from rushing down and causing pressure in the brain.

*Without its special circulatory system, a giraffe would not be able to lower its head for a drink of water.*

# Water Intake

Giraffes can survive several days without drinking water. This is an important adaptation because water is not always available in the giraffes' natural habitat. Instead, giraffes rely on the natural water content of their food and the morning dew.

# More Special Adaptations

## Feet

A giraffe's feet are large and heavy. They are about 12 inches (30 cm) long by 9 inches (23 cm) wide. Each foot has two hoofed toes. The hooves are wedge-shaped, thinning out toward the back of the foot.

## Head

Giraffes have long, flexible tongues that they use for pulling leaves from trees. Their tongues are approximately 18 inches (45 cm) long. Their tongues and lips are **prehensile** to help them pluck leaves. A giraffe's favorite leaves are from the acacia tree, which has many thorns and rough branches. To protect the face when eating, giraffes' lips are covered with hair. They can also close their nostrils when they want to, and their eyes have long eyelashes.

## Horns

The "horns" on a giraffe's head are not true horns. They are made of bone and are covered with skin and hair. Most horns are covered with a material similar to human fingernails. The tops of the giraffe's horns are rounded, not sharp. They can be up to 9 inches (23 cm) long and 6 inches (15 cm) around. Both male and female giraffes have two horns, but those of a female are smaller and thinner. Giraffes may also have a knoblike structure between their eyes. This is called the median horn. Males often have other bone growths on their heads. These help protect the giraffe from injury. When giraffes are born, their horns are made out of cartilage. A young giraffe's horns lie flat against its head until a few days after birth. As they grow, the cartilage is replaced by bone.

*A giraffe's tongue can be up to 2 feet (61 cm) long.*

## Hearing

A giraffe can hear at least as well as a human and probably better. To listen to a particular sound, a giraffe will turn in the direction the noise is coming from and perk its ears forward.

## Sight

Giraffes have excellent eyesight, and because of their height, they can see farther than other land mammals. They have been reported to be able to see a person 1 mile (1.6 km) away. Like other animals, giraffes are more likely to see something that moves, rather than something standing still. Giraffes are also able to tell the difference between colors.

Giraffes need their good vision to help protect themselves against predators. Lions and other predators are more likely to attack when they can surprise their prey. Often the whole herd will stand facing the lion with their heads up. A watchful herd of giraffes is not an easy target.

*A giraffe uses its keen sight and hearing to monitor its surroundings.*

# Ancestors and Relatives

Giraffes are now found only in Africa, but their ancestors probably lived in Asia and Europe as well. *Prolibytherium* and *Zarafa*, two ancestors of the giraffe, lived about 25 million years ago. *Sivatherium*, a more recent ancestor, lived in Africa and Asia five million years ago. *Sivatherium* had a heavy build, and stood 16 feet (4.9 m) tall. Unlike the giraffe, the *Sivatherium* usually had four horns that were branched like antlers. The neck and legs of *Sivatherium* were shorter than those of today's giraffe.

Scientists currently group giraffes with other animals that have an even number of toes on their hooves. These animals include pigs, camels, deer, hippopotamuses, antelopes, cattle, goats, sheep, and okapis.

The okapi is the giraffe's closest living relative. Okapis can grow to around 5.5 feet (1.7 m) tall. They weigh about 700 pounds (318 kg). An okapi's tongue is so long that it can lick its own eyes. Okapis live in forested areas and seem to communicate by sound more than giraffes do.

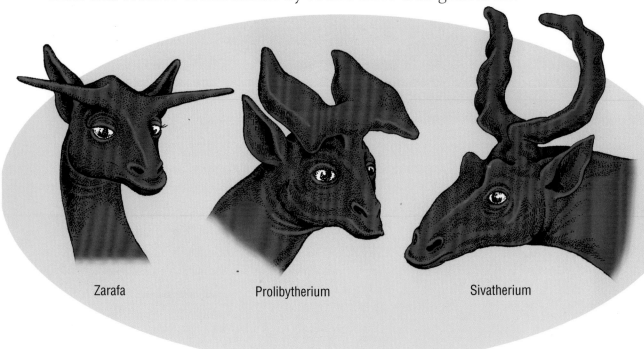

Zarafa          Prolibytherium          Sivatherium

*Giraffes have evolved over time, adapting themselves to suit their environment.*

# Species and Subspecies

Every known animal has been given a scientific name to describe it. This means that biologists from all over the world, who speak different languages and have different common names for animals, will understand which animal is being discussed. Since there is only one species of giraffe, the scientific name used for all giraffes is the same: *Giraffa camelopardalis*. Each word following *Giraffa camelopardalis* describes which subspecies of giraffe it is.

Each subspecies has its individual differences.

## SUBSPECIES

**Giraffes can be grouped into the following nine subspecies:**

| Common Name | Scientific Name |
| --- | --- |
| Reticulated giraffe | *Giraffa camelopardalis reticulata* |
| Nubian (or northern) giraffe | *Giraffa camelopardalis camelopardalis* |
| Kordofan giraffe | *Giraffa camelopardalis antiquorum* |
| Nigerian giraffe | *Giraffa camelopardalis peralta* |
| Rothschild's giraffe | *Giraffa camelopardalis rothschildi* |
| Masai giraffe | *Giraffa camelopardalis tippelskirchi* |
| Thornicroft's giraffe | *Giraffa camelopardalis thornicrofti* |
| Angolan giraffe | *Giraffa camelopardalis angolensis* |
| Cape (or southern) giraffe | *Giraffa camelopardalis giraffa* |

# The Herd

**Today most herds are made up of fewer than 20 giraffes.**

*Opposite: A herd of giraffes is not a set group. Individuals come and go frequently.*

Even though giraffes are often found alone or in pairs, they also form herds. Adult male giraffes tend to travel alone looking for females to mate with. Females and young giraffes usually stick together in a herd. When a female is found alone, she is often pregnant and has moved away from a herd to give birth.

Giraffes form herds of many different sizes. Pairs or small herds of giraffes are more common than large herds. Very large herds of 76 to 154 giraffes were reported in 1868, before people began to destroy the giraffe's natural habitat. Today most herds are made up of fewer than 20 giraffes.

*Giraffes are social animals and are not territorial. Their herds have no leaders.*

# Communication

Giraffes are very quiet animals, even during most social interactions. Giraffes communicate with each other by touching. A giraffe may use its nose to touch another giraffe on the body, neck, or head. A giraffe will also lick another's body, neck, mane, or horns. These behaviors may help giraffes form bonds with each other. For example, when a newborn giraffe joins a herd for the first time, the other adults nose the newborn.

A giraffe will threaten another giraffe or show **dominance** by standing up straight with chin and head held high. An outstretched neck and stiff-legged approach is another way giraffes show that they are a threat. A giraffe that is defending itself or is showing that it is submissive to another giraffe will lower its head and ears. It will jump away and leave the area when the other giraffe approaches.

Giraffes communicate danger by running away. Often the other members of the herd will stampede before they even know what the danger is.

*Giraffes sometimes rub their heads on one another's body or neck. Giraffes that are standing will sometimes rub their legs against the back of a giraffe that is lying down.*

# Sounds

For many years, people thought giraffes could not make any vocal sounds. Although they are usually silent, giraffes do make a variety of sounds. Female giraffes may whistle to call their young. They may also make a roaring bellow. Young giraffes may moo or bleat when they are left alone.

A startled, annoyed, or hungry giraffe may grunt or snort. Male giraffes sometimes make a coughing sound during mating. Zoo giraffes may bellow when they are hungry. Giraffes have also been reported to moan, snort, growl, scream, sneeze, hiss, snore, and make a flutelike sound.

*Giraffes communicate with each other both vocally and non-vocally.*

# Calves

**A calf usually stands up on its wobbly legs about 20 minutes after it is born.**

Young giraffes are called calves. A female giraffe usually gives birth to and raises one calf at a time. Twins are sometimes born, but not often. A calf usually stands up on its wobbly legs about 20 minutes after it is born. It will start to nurse about one hour later.

Calves are vulnerable to predators. For the first few weeks of life, calves spend half of the day and most of the night lying hidden. When a calf is frightened, it lowers its head, which helps it hide.

*Opposite: Giraffe calves are watched closely by other giraffes and are rarely left unattended.*

*Right: Giraffes are born in special areas called calving grounds. These grounds are usually in the bush, where the calves can be hidden from predators.*

# Mating

*Male giraffes may roam long distances in search of a mate.*

A female giraffe, or cow, comes into **heat** for one day every two weeks until she becomes pregnant. This is the only time that she will allow a male, or bull, to mate with her. Adult bull giraffes travel alone from herd to herd in search of a female in heat. Males may begin mating when they are about three and a half years old, but most are much older. Young males are prevented from mating by mature bulls.

Females can become pregnant for the first time when they are about three and a half years old. The **gestation period** for giraffes is about 15 months. A female giraffe has her first calf when she is about 5 years old. She will then have others about every 20 months.

A female giraffe can become pregnant within a few months after giving birth to a calf, even while she is still nursing that calf. A female can produce calves until she is about 20 years old and have as many as ten calves in her lifetime.

# Care

A mother giraffe keeps her newborn calf alone with her for the first weeks of its life. Mothers can be very protective of their young and usually remain no more than 82 feet (25 m) away from the calf during this time. They have been known to charge at people and at predators to protect their newborns. Giraffe mothers even keep other giraffes away during these first few weeks.

By the time the calf is 1 month old, the mother allows it to play with other young giraffes and to be near older giraffes. Groups of calves are sometimes left with one or more adult females who watch over the young so that the mothers may travel in search of food or water.

After the first 6 weeks of life, a calf may be away from its mother for many hours. Calves can go without nursing for long periods of time once they reach this age. Giraffe milk has about three times the amount of fat that cow milk does and helps sustain the calf during the long periods between feedings. The high fat content also helps the giraffe grow quickly.

*Even within the safe environment of a zoo, giraffe mothers keep their young close.*

# Development

## Birth to 4 Months

A calf is born with its front feet and head first. Giraffe mothers give birth standing up, and the calf will fall about 6.5 feet (2 m) to the ground. Newborns weigh 150 to 225 pounds (68 to 102 kg) and stand 6 feet (1.8 m) tall. The neck of a newborn giraffe is relatively shorter than that of an adult. In the first few months, calves grow quickly—up to 9 inches (23 cm) in a single week. The hair of a newborn is soft and short, and their horns lie pressed against the head. In a short time, however, the horns become raised.

*A small tuft of hair indicates where a newborn's horns are.*

## 4 Months to 2 Years

Life can be quite dangerous for young giraffes. Lions and spotted hyenas kill many calves. Three out of four young giraffes die before they are 1 year old. Although a calf will nurse for about nine months, it will feed on leaves after about 1 month of age. The calves grow quickly in their first year. At 6 months a young giraffe may reach almost 10 feet (3 m). By 1 year of age, they will have grown 43 inches (110 cm). By the time it reaches 2 years of age, the young giraffe will become completely independent.

*Calves are a food source not only for hyenas but for **scavengers**, such as vultures, as well.*

# 2 to 7 Years

After 2 years of age, a giraffe's growth rate will decrease. By the age of 5, female giraffes reach about 13 feet (4 m) tall. Male giraffes continue to grow until they are about 7 years old and reach about 16 feet (5 m) in height.

*As a giraffe matures, it spends more and more time away from its mother.*

# Habitat

**Giraffes can go for long periods without water, so their habitat is not as restricted as many other African animals.**

In the wild, giraffes live mainly in central and southern Africa. They tend to live in areas where there are enough trees and bushes for them to eat, but not so many that they block their view of predators. Males, and females without young, tend to live in more heavily forested areas. Females with young live in the open areas.

Since giraffes can go for long periods without water, their habitat is not as restricted as many other African animals. This allows them to travel farther in search of favorable grazing grounds.

*Opposite: Giraffes tend to stay close to their primary food source, the acacia tree.*

*Above: An open plain provides giraffes with a good vantage point.*

# Home Ranges

A giraffe's **home range** can be as small as 2 square miles (5 sq km) and as large as 262 square miles (679 sq km). The home range of a female giraffe averages about 24 square miles (62 sq km). Male home ranges average about 33 square miles (86 sq km). Males have larger home ranges because they travel farther, in search of females to mate with. Males also spend more time in forested areas that are dangerous for a female with a calf.

Giraffes once lived across the Sahara and in northern Africa, toward the Mediterranean Sea. Now they are found only in eastern and southern Africa, with a few groups in the west. Like many other species, giraffes are decreasing in number because their natural habitat is disappearing.

*Giraffes can be found in scattered groups across the African savanna.*

*Many animals, including the zebra, share the giraffe's habitat.*

# Seasonal Activities

Giraffe habitats generally have two seasons, one rainy and one dry. During the rainy or growing season, food and water are plentiful. At this time of year, giraffes eat mostly **deciduous leaves**, which they prefer. Giraffes also spread out and move farther away from water sources.

During the dry season, they eat leaves from evergreens and other types of plants. They spend more time hunting for food, and they have less time to rest. Although calves can be born at any time of the year, they are usually born in the dry season, when herds are less likely to move around.

Even though giraffes can survive a long time without drinking water, they tend to stay near water during the dry season. This is partly because the plants growing by water usually produce better leaves.

# Walking and Galloping

The giraffe has only two ways of moving from one place to another. It either walks or gallops. During the day, when they do most of their eating, giraffes walk quite slowly. They travel only about 0.1 miles (0.2 km) per hour. Lone males tend to travel farther and faster.

A giraffe can travel at a gallop for long distances without getting tired. The record running speed of this tallest of animals is 35 miles (56.3 km) per hour. Giraffes will gallop away when they are being chased, and they sometimes gallop away from things that frighten them. Male giraffes will chase off other males at a gallop. Unfamiliar sights or encounters, like airplanes flying overhead, will cause giraffes to stampede, until they get used to them. Giraffes that live near Nairobi International Airport are now so used to airplanes that they do not even look up when they fly overhead. When they were regularly shot by hunters, giraffes would gallop away if a person came close. Today in protected areas, giraffes familiar with tourists are much less likely to gallop off when a person approaches, especially if the person is in a vehicle.

When a giraffe walks, it puts all its weight first on its left legs and then on its right legs. Its neck moves back and forth in rhythm to help keep the giraffe balanced.

When a giraffe gallops, it moves its back legs together as a pair and its front legs as a pair. The back feet land outside and ahead of the front feet. They hold their tails curled on their rumps.

# *On the Track of a Giraffe*

In the wild, the easiest way to find giraffes is to look for their distinct shape. Because of their height, they can be seen from a great distance. Some scientists report that it is easier to see giraffes' heads over tops of trees than it is to spot their legs and bodies nearer the ground. Giraffes are very well camouflaged. Some of these other signs will let you know if giraffes are in the area.

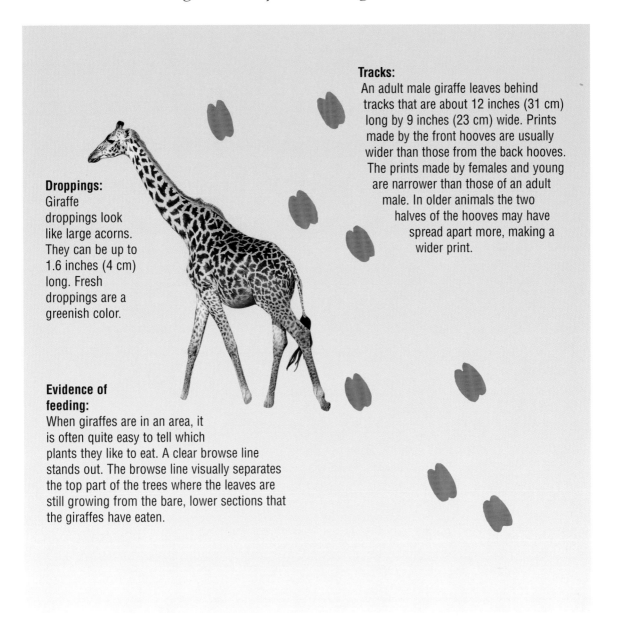

**Tracks:**
An adult male giraffe leaves behind tracks that are about 12 inches (31 cm) long by 9 inches (23 cm) wide. Prints made by the front hooves are usually wider than those from the back hooves. The prints made by females and young are narrower than those of an adult male. In older animals the two halves of the hooves may have spread apart more, making a wider print.

**Droppings:**
Giraffe droppings look like large acorns. They can be up to 1.6 inches (4 cm) long. Fresh droppings are a greenish color.

**Evidence of feeding:**
When giraffes are in an area, it is often quite easy to tell which plants they like to eat. A clear browse line stands out. The browse line visually separates the top part of the trees where the leaves are still growing from the bare, lower sections that the giraffes have eaten.

# Food

The giraffe is an **herbivore**, which means that it feeds on plants. Herbivores tend to spend much of their time eating in order to get enough nutrients to live. Because a giraffe is such a large animal, it needs to eat plenty of food to survive. Giraffes spend more time eating than doing any other activity. A giraffe spends about 16 to 20 hours each day feeding.

Giraffes are **browsers,** which means that they eat parts of trees and shrubs. Other herbivores are grazers, which means they eat grass. An adult giraffe eats up to 74 pounds (34 kg) of leaves in a day.

*Opposite: A giraffe will spend much of its day eating and in search of food.*

*Above: Although giraffes eat mostly leaves and shoots, they will also feed on flowers, vines, and herbs.*

# What They Eat

A giraffe's favorite food is the leaves from thorny acacia trees and bushes. Even though they prefer acacia leaves, wild giraffes will eat from more than one hundred different species of plants. Giraffes usually eat the leaves and small twigs from large shrubs, trees, and vines. They sometimes eat bark, thorns, ants, flowers, and fruits. To get the minerals they need, giraffes will also eat salt or salty soil. Giraffes have even been seen eating meat off dead animals, but this is not common.

When giraffes browse on trees, they eat above the level where antelopes can reach. Antelopes can eat leaves as high as 7 feet (2.1 m) above the ground. Giraffes eat from that point up to about 16 feet (4.8 m).

*Different species of acacia plants are found in many different countries. In Australia, where there are no large browsing animals, the acacia trees have no thorns. It is likely that one of the main reasons acacias have grown thorns in Africa is to help protect them from giraffes.*

# How They Eat

To eat, a giraffe stretches its tongue out and wraps it around the tip of a branch. It pulls the branch through its outstretched lips and closes its mouth. Then it pulls its head away, combing the leaves into its mouth with its lower front teeth. It uses its flat molars at the back of its mouth to chew. Giraffes have thick, rubbery saliva. This helps prevent the sharp acacia thorns from pricking the tongue or insides of the mouth.

Giraffes chew their cud like cows do. This is called **ruminating**, or cudding. After a giraffe eats, it brings the food up again and chews it a second time. This helps break down the tough plant material for better digestion. When a giraffe is not eating, it spends much of its time chewing its cud. A giraffe can chew its cud while it is walking, standing still, or lying down.

*Giraffes eat mostly in the early morning and late afternoon.*
*In the early afternoon, they spend more time ruminating.*

# Water

To drink water in the wild, a giraffe must lower its head all the way down to the ground. To do this it must either bend its knees forward or spread its front legs wide apart. It will remain bent down drinking for short periods, usually 20 to 60 seconds. When giraffes are drinking, they are an easy target for lions. If a group of giraffes are at a water hole, some will usually stay upright while the others drink. This may be so they can watch for predators.

Giraffes are able to last many days without drinking water. The leaves that a giraffe eats can provide it with much of the moisture it needs. If a giraffe is feeding on fresh leaves, it may be able to live for months without drinking any water. If water is available, however, giraffes may drink every day. In zoos, a giraffe may drink 10 gallons (45.4 L) per day in hot weather.

*Like all animals, giraffes need water to survive.*

# The Food Cycle

A food cycle shows how energy, in the form of food, is passed from one living thing to another. Giraffes get energy by eating plants. In turn, giraffes provide energy to other animals in their environment.

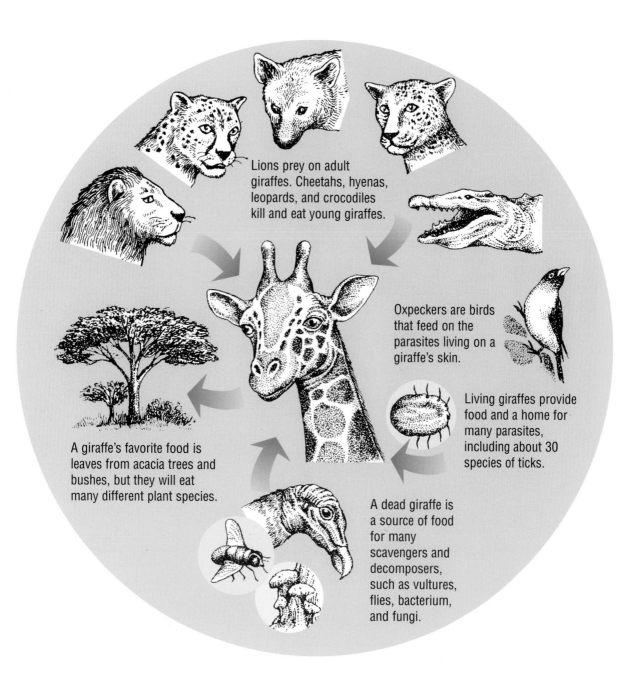

Lions prey on adult giraffes. Cheetahs, hyenas, leopards, and crocodiles kill and eat young giraffes.

Oxpeckers are birds that feed on the parasites living on a giraffe's skin.

Living giraffes provide food and a home for many parasites, including about 30 species of ticks.

A giraffe's favorite food is leaves from acacia trees and bushes, but they will eat many different plant species.

A dead giraffe is a source of food for many scavengers and decomposers, such as vultures, flies, bacterium, and fungi.

# Competition

**Lions attack and kill giraffes of all ages and sizes.**

*Opposite: The giraffe lives peaceably with most animals.*

The adult giraffe has few enemies. Besides humans, the main predators of giraffes are lions. Lions attack and kill giraffes of all ages and sizes.

Attacking a giraffe can be dangerous, even for a lion. Adult giraffes often kick out at lions when they or their young are attacked. There have been several reports of giraffes killing lions by kicking them or by trampling on them.

Cheetahs, hyenas, leopards, and even crocodiles may occasionally kill giraffes, but they prefer small giraffes. A full-grown giraffe has little to fear from these predators.

Humans, too, have proven to be a dangerous enemy. They have hunted giraffes, given them diseases through contact with domesticated livestock, and destroyed large parts of their habitat.

*Lions are the giraffe's main predator, but even they can be hurt by a giraffe's powerful kick.*

# Competing with Other Giraffes

Male giraffes sometimes fight with each other. Most fights are to determine which male is dominant or which one will mate with a female. Males fight with their necks, heads, and horns in a type of fighting called necking. Their heads are extremely large and heavy. A giraffe's head alone can weigh more than 55 pounds (25 kg) and be 27 inches (68.6 cm) long.

During a fight, one giraffe will lower its head and swing it at the other giraffe. The other giraffe will try to move out of the way and then will swing back. The giraffes try to hit each other with their horns. Because their horns are blunt, these matches appear to be harmless. In very rare cases, however, they result in a giraffe getting seriously injured or even killed. Even in very serious necking matches, the giraffes never bite or kick each other.

*In a competition between giraffes, the neck is the largest and most vulnerable target.*

# Teamwork

Giraffes tend to ignore other species that browse or graze with them. Animals, such as zebra and wildebeest, feed near giraffes to take advantage of the giraffes' good eyesight and vantage points. Two species of birds, the red-billed oxpecker and the yellow-billed oxpecker, will often ride on the giraffes and eat ticks from the giraffes' skin. While searching for ticks, the birds remove dirt and dry skin. These birds also remove maggots from any wounds and alert giraffes to predators by flying away when alarmed.

*Oxpeckers are companions to many other animals as well, including the water buffalo.*

# Conflicts with Humans

Throughout history people have hunted giraffes. The giraffe's tail has thick, nylon-like hairs. These hairs are used for sewing and to make fly switches, bracelets, necklaces, and decorations. Fresh giraffe meat can be eaten or dried. The dried meat is either chewed dry or soaked before cooking. The hide has been used to make shields, shoes, whips, pots, and drum coverings. Leg tendons can be used for guitar strings and sewing thread.

Today, giraffes are protected in most countries. However, illegal hunters called **poachers** are still a problem. Not only do they kill giraffes directly, they also hurt many other giraffes that may then die from their injuries. Poachers set wire snares that remain around a giraffe's legs after they have pulled away. Giraffes in this condition may die later of blood poisoning, or be so weakened that they easily fall prey to lions.

*Humans have impacted the habitats of many African animals, including the giraffe.*

# Disease

Aside from hunting, humans have also caused giraffe populations to drop by using up their natural habitat for farming and development. Farms have also brought disease. In the late 1800s, a disease called **rinderpest** first appeared in Africa. It was brought there when domestic cows were shipped to Africa to feed foreign soldiers. This deadly virus soon spread from the cows to giraffes. Hundreds of giraffes died from the disease, and others were temporarily blinded, making them easy targets for lions. This was only the first of several outbreaks of rinderpest in Africa. In 1960, another outbreak in northern Kenya killed about 40 percent of the giraffes there.

*Domestic cows have been known to spread the deadly rinderpest virus to giraffes.*

# Folklore

Throughout history, giraffes have been described as having features that combine those of other animals. The ancient Romans thought the giraffe looked like a cross between a camel and a leopard. This was because it had a long neck and two-toed hooves like a camel and spots like a leopard. In the first century A.D., a giraffe was described as a combination of a horse, an ox, and a camel. In 1022, an Arab geographer suggested that giraffes were produced when male panthers mated with female camels. Another scholar said giraffes were produced by a female camel, a male hyena, and a wild cow.

Recently the giraffe has been seen as a symbol of goodness. The Giraffe Project was started by Ann Medlock in 1982. The project honors people who "stick their necks out" to help other people. The organization sees the giraffe as a perfect role model: it has a big heart; it is an herbivore, so it does not eat other creatures; and it is silent, but with the strength to fight a lion if necessary.

*Opposite: The scientific name for giraffes is* Giraffa camelopardalis, *which comes from the ancient Roman belief that the giraffe looked like a camel.*

*The Giraffe Project is now run by Ann Medlock and her husband, John Graham.*

# *Folktales*

Wildlife plays an important role in African folklore and folktales. Most folktales about giraffes focus on how they became so different from other animals. Many of these stories explain how the giraffe got its special characteristics.

## Magic and the Giraffe

This story is about how the giraffe was created. In this tale, an antelope saves a man's life. In return the man uses his magic to make the antelope big and strong, with long legs and a long neck so it can reach the juiciest leaves. The new animal was called a giraffe.

Bond, Neil (illustrator). *How the Giraffe Became a Giraffe: A Traditional Story.* Toronto: Prentice Hall Ginn Canada, 1996.

## Growing Tall

"Why the Giraffe Has a Long Neck" is an East African fable. It also explains why the rhinoceros has such a bad temper. A rhino and a giraffe decide they both want long necks to reach up to the treetops. When Rhino is late for a meeting with a witch doctor, he misses out on the special potion that makes necks grow. Giraffe gets both of their shares, and his neck and legs grow long enough to reach the tallest branches.

Greaves, Nick. *When Hippo was Hairy and Other Tales from Africa.* Hauppage, New York: Barron's Educational Series, 1998.

## Making Patterns

This story explains how the giraffe, the zebra, and the leopard got their markings. At first, the giraffe, the zebra, and the leopard are all one color with no markings on their coats. To escape being hunted by people and leopards, the giraffe and the zebra hide in a forest. By standing in the patchy shadows of the forest, the giraffe becomes all blotchy, and the zebra becomes striped. The leopard then gets spots so that he will be difficult to see while he is hunting. These three animals have kept those patterns ever since.

Kipling, Rudyard. *How the Leopard Got His Spots (Just So Stories).* London: MacMillan's Children's Books, 1980.

## Giraffe Hunters

Some tales show the giraffe as an animal of moral virtue. In "The Giraffe Hunters," told by the Masai people, a hunter named Kume finds a large and impressive giraffe that he wants to kill. He goes back to the village to get his friend Lumbwa to help him. They make a plan. Kume will hide in a tree to wait for the giraffe to return to feed. He will then jump on the giraffe to surprise him, and Lumbwa will kill him with his bow. However, when

Kume lands on the giraffe, it starts to gallop, and Lumbwa is overcome with laughter at the sight of his friend riding a giraffe. He fails to use his bow, and the giraffe gallops off with Kume. Eventually Kume kills the giraffe with a knife, but then he refuses to share his kill with Lumbwa. In the end, Kume loses the whole giraffe because he refused to share with his friend.

Courlander, Harold. *The King's Drum and Other African Stories.* New York: Harcourt, Brace & World, 1962.

# Myths vs. Facts

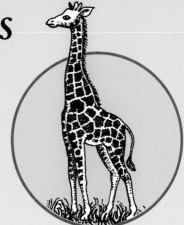

*A giraffe's front legs are much longer than its back legs.*

The slope of a giraffe's back makes its front legs appear much longer than its back legs. In fact, all four of its legs are about the same length. The front legs are only one-tenth longer than the back legs.

*Giraffes are gentle and harmless.*

Although giraffes rarely attack other animals, they will defend themselves when threatened. Giraffes kick with enormous power. They have killed attacking lions by kicking them in the head.

*Giraffes always sleep standing up.*

Although giraffes occasionally sleep standing up, they usually lie down. To sleep deeply, a giraffe bends its head back alongside its body and rests it on the ground. During one night, an adult giraffe might do this five times, sleeping for about three or four minutes each time.

# Tell a Tall Tale

Folk stories often provide an explanation for things that can be seen in the world, such as the fact that giraffes are tall. Write your own folktale that explains an observation or fact about giraffes. Invent your own explanation for why the giraffe's neck is so long, or how the giraffe got its color pattern. A few story starters are offered below. Use one of them to start your tale, or make up your own. Be sure to base your story on a fact or observation about giraffes.

**1** Giraffe once had large horns like Antelope. Then one day Giraffe and Antelope went into the forest...

**2** Okapi and Giraffe were brothers. One day when they were grazing on the plains...

**3** Giraffe was once the noisiest animal in Africa.

**4** The herbivores called an emergency meeting. Lion had killed one of their herd again last night. Something had to be done.

# Giraffe Distribution in Africa

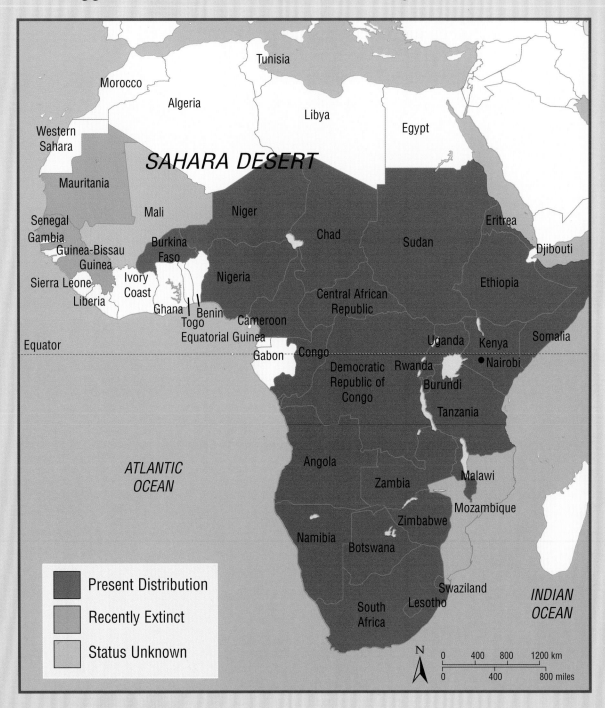

Tunisia
Morocco
Algeria
Libya
Egypt
Western Sahara
*SAHARA DESERT*
Mauritania
Mali
Niger
Chad
Sudan
Eritrea
Senegal
Gambia
Burkina Faso
Djibouti
Guinea-Bissau
Guinea
Nigeria
Central African Republic
Ethiopia
Sierra Leone
Ivory Coast
Liberia
Ghana
Benin
Togo
Cameroon
Equatorial Guinea
Equator
Uganda
Kenya
Somalia
Gabon
Congo
Democratic Republic of Congo
Rwanda
Burundi
Nairobi
*ATLANTIC OCEAN*
Tanzania
Angola
Zambia
Malawi
Mozambique
Zimbabwe
Namibia
Botswana
Swaziland
Lesotho
*INDIAN OCEAN*
South Africa

Present Distribution
Recently Extinct
Status Unknown

N

| 0 | 400 | 800 | 1200 km |
| 0 | | 400 | 800 miles |

# *Status*

**Today, giraffes are found in Africa, south of the Sahara Desert.**

*Opposite: Giraffes can still be found in most parts of Africa.*

Giraffes were found throughout Africa 10,000 years ago. Later, giraffes became extinct in North Africa as the climate changed and most of the area became a desert. Giraffes became extinct in Egypt about 4,000 years ago and in Morocco about 1,400 years ago.

Today, giraffes are found in Africa, south of the Sahara Desert. In 1998, the World Conservation Union (IUCN) suggested that there were more than 110,000 giraffes in Africa. This included the almost 50,000 giraffes living in and around protected areas. There are about 1,000 giraffes living in captivity throughout the world.

*The giraffe population today is considered stable, but it still requires the efforts of conservation programs.*

# Hunting and Conserving Giraffes

For hunters with guns, a giraffe is an easy target. Thousands of giraffes were slaughtered by early hunters, settlers, and explorers in Africa. The giraffe was a special target for "big game" hunters. These hunters often wrote about their kills. They mentioned chasing the giraffe as being the best part of the hunt. They admired its unusual and distinctive way of galloping. But some hunters questioned how "sporting" it was to kill a giraffe.

Frederick Vaughan Kirby, a British hunter, wrote in 1896: "One can scarcely consider it an elevating form of sport...for it calls forth neither endurance, courage, nor extraordinary skill on the part of the hunter." He thought that all giraffe hunting should be stopped or the animals would be hunted to extinction.

People seemed to recognize the need to protect the giraffe. It was one of the first animals to be protected, in southern Africa, in 1893. Other countries soon followed. Under the London Convention of 1900, giraffes were listed as a protected species. After the London Convention of 1933, national parks were set up to protect African wildlife, including the giraffe.

*Much of Africa's wildlife has found refuge in conservation parks.*

# *Viewpoints*

## Should hunters be allowed to shoot giraffes?

Although some African countries prohibit giraffe hunting, others sell licenses to hunt the animal. Licenses can cost $5,000 or more. Farmers are sometimes permitted to shoot giraffes that are damaging their crops or fences. Although very few giraffes are killed this way, many people feel that hunting wild giraffes should be stopped.

**PRO**

**1** Proper licensing procedures may result in less illegal hunting.

**2** Money raised from licenses can be used for conservation projects to help giraffes.

**3** The few giraffes killed in this way may not affect the population, especially in areas where the giraffe population is stable or increasing.

**CON**

**1** Poachers continue to kill giraffes, even in countries with licensed hunting systems.

**2** Very little money is raised through licensing, compared to that raised by tourism, in the wildlife parks.

**3** In recent years, the balance of giraffe populations has become more stable. Hunting would upset this balance and cause the decline of the giraffe species.

*Betty Leslie-Melville has devoted her life to protecting the giraffe population in Africa.*

# Relocating Giraffes

In the early 1970s, a group of 130 Rothschild's giraffes living on a large cattle ranch in western Kenya were in trouble. The government decided to divide the ranch into small plots and move people into the area. This would leave no room for the giraffes.

Betty and Jock Leslie-Melville founded the African Fund for Endangered Wildlife to raise money to move the giraffes. Betty is an American living in Nairobi, Kenya, and her husband Jock was a Kenyan citizen originally from Great Britain. With their help, four groups of giraffes were relocated to national parks where they could live more safely.

Betty and Jock also moved some young Rothschild's giraffes to their home in Nairobi. The first giraffe, Daisy, became one of the most famous giraffes in history. A book was written about her (*Raising Daisy Rothschild*), and a television movie was made about her life (*The Last Giraffe*). Daisy died in 1989, but other Rothschild's giraffes still live at the Leslie-Melville home.

Now called Giraffe Manor, the home is an educational center open to the public. Giraffe Manor is run by the African Fund for Endangered Wildlife. Every year, 30,000 to 40,000 African schoolchildren visit the center free of charge to learn about animal conservation. More than 30,000 others visit the center every year as well.

The giraffes living at Giraffe Manor are very friendly and comfortable around people. The lands surrounding Giraffe Manor are protected. The giraffe sanctuary now includes more than 100 acres (40.5 ha).

After Jock's death in the mid-1980s, Betty continued this work with her son. She was awarded a Safari Planet Earth Award in 1994 for her efforts in environmental protection and education.

Plans to relocate more wild Rothschild's giraffes are underway. One goal is to help the individuals of different groups breed with each other. This helps the animals remain healthy by seeing that more matings between unrelated giraffes take place. Another goal is the **reintroduction** of some Rothschild's giraffes to parts of Uganda. Thanks to the efforts of people like Jock and Betty, more than 350 Rothschild's giraffes now live in safe areas in Kenya.

*The giraffes at Giraffe Manor both entertain and educate their guests.*

# Wildlife Biologists Talk About Giraffes

## Bristol Foster

*"Each year of study revealed the fascinating adaptations that have allowed giraffes to survive for millions of years."*
Dr. Foster is a wildlife ecologist who has spent many years studying giraffes in Nairobi National Park in Kenya.

## Anne Innis Dagg

*"Today most of the countries in Africa protect their giraffes by laws which punish all poachers....*
*Eventually, because of human population pressures, the giraffe will likely be restricted to national parks and game reserves in Africa."*
Dr. Dagg has studied giraffe behavior and ecology in the wild in Africa. She has also studied the heredity and behavior of zoo giraffes.

## Richard Despard Estes

*"The giraffe is not only physically but also socially aloof, forming no lasting bonds with its fellows and associating in the most casual way with other individuals whose ranges overlap its own."*
Dr. Estes has studied many large African mammals and has written a field guide about their behavior.

# Current Status

The World Conservation Union now classifies giraffes as lower risk and conservation dependent. This means that giraffes are not considered to be endangered or vulnerable. However, if current programs to protect giraffes are stopped, giraffes would be considered endangered or vulnerable within five years. The biggest threat to giraffes today is poaching.

Today, the total number of giraffes is considered stable. Decreases in some populations are balanced by increases in others. Decreases in the northern and western parts of their ranges are mainly due to poaching. In western and central African countries, giraffes live in small, scattered populations, and their numbers continue to decrease. In eastern and southern Africa, giraffes are widespread. In the southern parts of their range, giraffe numbers are increasing due to effective protection provided by parks, reserves, and private landowners.

*The efforts of conservationists have helped rebuild
and maintain the giraffe numbers in Africa.*

# What You Can Do

You can help giraffes by learning about them and teaching others what you have learned. You can also help by becoming involved with organizations that work to protect them and their natural habitat. Write to one of these organizations to find out what you can do to protect giraffes and other wildlife.

## Conservation Groups

### INTERNATIONAL

International Union for Conservation of Nature and Natural Resources (IUCN)
World Conservation Union
28 rue Mauvernes
CH-1196 Gland
Switzerland

World Wide Fund for Nature-International
Avenue du Mont Blanc
CH-1196 Gland
Switzerland

### AFRICA

The East African Wild Life Society
P. O. Box 20110
Nairobi, Kenya

Tanzania National Park
P. O. Box 3134
Arusha, Tanzania

### UNITED STATES

African Fund for Endangered Wildlife
4602 Waterfall Court
Owings Mills, MD
21117

African Wildlife Foundation
1400 Sixteenth Street NW
Suite 120
Washington, DC
20036

World Wildlife Fund
1250 24th Street NW
Washington, DC
20037-1175

### CANADA

World Wildlife Fund
245 Eglinton Ave. East
Suite 410
Toronto, Ontario
M4P 3J1

# Twenty Fascinating Facts

**1** The Egyptian symbol for giraffe means "to tell the future."

**2** Camels have the same unusual way of walking as giraffes.

**3** Giraffes are good jumpers and are not slowed down by cattle fences even 4 feet (1.2 m) high.

**4** Giraffes are one of the only animals born with horns. The horns get bonier with age.

**5** A giraffe's heart beats twice as fast as a cow's heart and six times as fast as an elephant's heart.

**6** In the early 1900s, many giraffes tore down telegraph wires after accidentally running into them. Officials eventually raised the height of the wires above the giraffe's reach.

**7** The giraffe was not named for its long neck, but for its walking speed. The word "giraffe" comes from the Arabic word *xirapha*, which means "one that walks very fast."

**8** A giraffe can move quite quickly. Even when it is walking, one stride can cover up to 15 feet (4.6 m).

**9** What appears to be a giraffe's "knee" is actually more like a human's wrist.

**10** From its hooves to the top of its head, a giraffe is one-third neck.

**11** Unlike horses, giraffes can reach almost any part of their body with their tail. This helps them keep pests away.

**12** Because a giraffe's neck is so long, it is possible to watch the movement of food up its throat and into its mouth when it brings up food to chew its cud.

**13** Giraffes have purple tongues to reflect UV light from the sun and prevent sunburn.

**14** It is not easy for a giraffe to lie down. First it gets down on its knees. Then its back end "sits" down. To get up, it does the opposite.

**15** The seeds of kameeldoring, a type of acacia, only begin to grow after passing through a giraffe's digestive system.

**16** Giraffes never lie on their sides. Their bodies need to be upright in order for their digestive system to work properly.

**17** A giraffe has 32 teeth. It has 12 in its upper jaw and 20 in its lower.

**18** A giraffe is the only mammal that can see almost all of its own body.

**19** Giraffes do not seem to be able to swim, so they avoid deep water.

**20** Research on the giraffe's circulatory system may help future space travelers. When astronauts reenter Earth's atmosphere, they can have serious problems with their circulatory systems. Researchers at NASA hope that studying how the giraffe's circulatory system works will help them to find a way to help astronauts.

# Glossary

**adaptations:** Changes made to fit into a certain environment

**browsers:** Herbivores that feed on parts of plants, such as leaves or small branches

**circulatory system:** The system of the heart and blood vessels that pumps blood through the body

**deciduous leaves:** Leaves that fall off during a specific season

**dominance:** The state of having control and authority

**gestation period:** The length of time a female is pregnant with young

**heat:** The period of time during which a female giraffe is ready and willing to mate with a male giraffe

**herbivore:** An animal that feeds on plants

**home range:** The entire area in which an individual lives

**necking:** When two giraffes hit each other repeatedly with their heads

**poachers:** Illegal hunters

**prehensile:** Specially adapted for gripping objects

**reintroduction:** When a group of individuals of a species are moved into an area where the species was previously found

**rinderpest:** A deadly virus that is spread from domestic cows to many other species, including giraffes

**ruminating:** Chewing the cud

**scavenger:** An animal that eats dead animals that it has not killed

# Suggested Reading

Arnold, Caroline. *Giraffe*. New York: William Morrow & Co. Inc., 1987.

Dagg, Anne Innis, and J. Bristol Foster. *The Giraffe: Its Biology, Behavior and Ecology*. Malabar, Florida: Robert E. Krieger Publishing Company, 1982.

Estes, R. D. *The Behavior Guide to African Mammals*. Berkeley: The University of California Press, 1991.

Leslie-Melville, Betty and Jock. *Raising Daisy Rothschild*. New York: Simon and Schuster, 1977.

Nowak, Ronald M. *Walker's Mammals of the World*. Sixth edition. Baltimore: Johns Hopkins University Press, 1999.

Sherr, Lynn. *Tall Blondes: A Book About Giraffes*. Kansas City: Andrews McMeel Publishing, 1997.

**GIRAFFES ON THE INTERNET**

One of the places you can find out more about giraffes is on the Internet. Visit the following sites, or try searching on your own:

**Sweet, Gentle Giraffes**
http://members.tripod.com/~randm2/giraffes.html

**Planet Giraffe**
http://www.planet-pets.com/pIntgraf.htm

**The Giraffe Centre**
http://www.giraffecentre.org/index.html

# Index